John D McPherson

The Evolution of the Myth

As exemplified in General Grant's history of the plot of President Polk and

Secretary Marcy to sacrifice two American armies in the Mexican war of

1846-1848

John D McPherson

The Evolution of the Myth
As exemplified in General Grant's history of the plot of President Polk and Secretary Marcy to sacrifice two American armies in the Mexican war of 1846-1848

ISBN/EAN: 9783744748261

Printed in Europe, USA, Canada, Australia, Japan

Cover: Foto ©ninafisch / pixelio.de

More available books at **www.hansebooks.com**

THE

EVOLUTION OF MYTH

AS EXEMPLIFIED IN

GENERAL GRANT'S HISTORY OF THE PLOT OF
PRESIDENT POLK AND SECRETARY MARCY
TO SACRIFICE TWO AMERICAN
ARMIES IN THE MEXICAN
WAR OF 1846-48.

BY SENEX.

WASHINGTON, D. C.
WILLIAM H. MORRISON.
1890.

The Evolution of Myth.

THE MYTH.

In the Personal Memoirs of General Grant, volume 1, chapter 9, under the heading of "Political Intrigue," are found the following paragraphs:

"The Mexican War was a political war, and the administration conducting it desired to make political capital out of it. General Scott was at the head of the Army, and being a soldier of acknowledged professional capacity, his claim to the command of the forces in the field was almost undisputable, and does not seem to have been denied by President Polk, or Marcy his Secretary of War. Scott was whig, and the administration was democratic. General Scott was also known to have political aspirations, and nothing so popularizes a candidate for high civil position as military victories. It would not do therefore to give him command of the 'Army of Invasion.' The plans submitted by Scott for a campaign in Mexico were disapproved by the administration, and he replied in a tone, possibly a little disrespectful, to the effect that if a soldier's plans were not to be supported by the administration, success could not be expected. This was on the 27th of May, 1846.

Four days later he (General Scott) was notified that
he need not go to Mexico. General Gaines was
next in rank, but he was too old and feeble to take
the field. Colonel Zachary Taylor a Brigadier
General by brevet was therefore left in command.
He too was a whig but was not supposed to entertain any political aspiration; nor did he; but after
the fall of Monterey, his third battle and third
complete victory, the whig papers at home began
to speak of him as the candidate of their party for
the presidency. Something had to be done to
neutralize his growing popularity. He could not
be relieved from duty in the field where all his
battles had been victories; the design would have
been too transparent. It was finally decided to
send General Scott to Mexico in chief command,
and to authorize him to carry out his own original
plan—that is to capture Vera Cruz and march upon
the capital of the country. It was no doubt supposed that Scott's ambition would lead him to
slaughter Taylor or destroy his chances for the
presidency, and yet it was hoped that he would
not make sufficient capital himself to secure the
prize.

"The administration had indeed a most em-
barrassing problem to solve. It was engaged in a
war of conquest which must be carried to a successful issue or the political object would be unattained. Yet all the capable officers of the requisite rank belonged to the opposition, and the man
selected for his lack of political ambition had himself become a prominent candidate for the presidency. It was necessary to destroy his chances
promptly. The fact is, the administration of Mr.
Polk made every preparation to disgrace General

Scott, or, to speak more correctly, to drive him to such desperation that he would disgrace himself. General Scott had opposed conquest by the way of the Rio Grande, Matamoras and Saltillo from the first. Now that he was in command of all the forces in Mexico, he withdrew from Taylor most of his regular troops and left him only enough volunteers, as he thought, to hold the line then in possession of the invading army. Indeed Scott did not deem it important to hold anything beyond the Rio Grande, and authorized Taylor to fall back to that line if he chose. Taylor protested against the depletion of his army, and his subsequent movement upon Buena Vista would indicate that he did not share the views of his chief in regard to the unimportance of conquest beyond the Rio Grande.

"Scott had estimated the men and material that would be required to capture Vera Cruz and to march on the capital of the country, 260 miles in the interior. He was promised all he asked, and seemed to have not only the confidence of the President, but his sincere good wishes. The promises were all broken. Only about half the troops were furnished that had been pledged, other war material was withheld, and Scott had scarcely started for Mexico before the President undertook to supersede him by the appointment of Senator Thomas H. Benton as Lieutenant General. This being refused by Congress, the President asked legislative authority to place a junior over a senior of the same grade, with a view of appointing Benton to the rank of Major General, and then placing him in command of the army; but Congress failed to accede to this proposition as well, and Scott remained in command; but every General appointed to serve under him was politically opposed to the chief, and several were personally hostile.''

In the next chapter it is said:

''General Scott had less than 12,000 men at Vera Cruz. He had been promised by the administration a very much larger force, or claimed that he had, and he was a man of veracity.''

And again:

'' It was very important to get the army away from Vera Cruz as soon as possible in order to avoid the yellow fever or vomito, which usually visits that city early in the year and is very fatal to persons not acclimated.''

There might be some uncertainty as to what is meant by slaughtering Taylor and disgracing Scott, if it were not rendered clear by the means used to effect these objects. Taylor and Scott were to be deprived of half the troops which the one had, and the other counted on. This explanation dispels all ambiguity. For unless it was the purpose of the administration to enhance the glory of these commanders by forcing them to win great victories with small armies, its only purpose must have been to have them defeated. In no other way could the diminution of his army in the face of an advancing enemy destroy Taylor's prospects

for the presidency, or the withholding of reinforcements from Scott, after he had landed at Vera
Cruz, prevent him from making political capital
by victory.

The story of this enormous wickedness, the more
enormous, that it was planned long in advance and
involved the destruction of ten thousand men with
the principal victim who was to be lured to his
death by hypocritical professions of confidence and
good wishes, is told with a circumstantiality and
fullness of detail that to most readers will supply
the place of proof. And it draws from the narrator
not a single expression of indignation or even of
disapproval.

Mr. Polk had been honored by the direct votes
of the people of his State and of the whole country,
with the highest offices, legislative and executive.
Mr. Marcy had been a Judge of the Supreme Court
of his State, Governor of the State, Senator of the
United States, and member of two cabinets, as
Secretary of War and Secretary of State, and yet,
says his biographer, his "crowning virtue was his
incorruptible integrity." These men had lived all
their lives in the fierce light of political life, and
had gone to the grave honored and respected by
all. And twenty years after the death of the last
survivor we are told by a President of the United

States, that these men had prostituted their high offices, had violated their oaths, and had conspired the defeat and destruction of the armies which they had sent to war in a foreign land, and all to advance the interests of their party at home !

That such a tale should be told at all is to be deplored, not only because it is false, but because, though it be false, it will tend powerfully to encourage political depravity. The vulgar villian needs no encouragement, or, if he does, will find it in the creed of his class, that "they all do it," and wants no proof that all men are alike corrupt. But those are more numerous who have some regard for virtue, some belief in disinterested patriotism, and who might shrink from voting for a scheme to plunder the public or from counting out an elected candidate, were there not held up before their eyes the example of men like Polk and Marcy, honored and esteemed, who yet had sacrificed conscience, violated duty, and perjured their souls for the good of their party.

And then surely, no more damaging charge was ever brought against free institutions than that the elect of the people entered into a plot to sacrifice the welfare of his country and the lives of ten thousand of his fellow-citizens in order to rid himself of a political rival. I venture to say no hereditary monarch ever did the like; and if a President of the United States has done this, he has supplied an unanswerable argument to those who maintain that, according to the experience of all ages and all countries, patriotism will never long continue to rise superior to the rage of party spirit and the allurements of ambition; and that only a hereditary ruler, whose fortunes and those of his children are indissolubly bound up with those of his country, can be relied on for unswerving devotion to its honor and interests.

Of course the charge is not true—could not be. For if Taylor's army had been overwhelmed at Buena Vista, or Scott's had perished of vomito while unable to get into Vera Cruz for want of a siege train, or out of it for want of reinforcements, the "war of conquest which must be carried to a successful issue" would have failed and the political object have been unattained. A more absurd story could not have been invented than that Polk and Marcy expected to conquer Mexico with the armies of Scott and Taylor, and at the same time withhold absolutely necessary reinforcements and supplies in order that the two generals should be slaughtered or disgraced. In a violent letter which General Scott, after the campaign, addressed to Governor Marcy (No. 43), he insinuated that he had not been properly supported—I shall recur to this further on—and the Secretary replied (No. 44),

in a few contemptuous sentences which should
have set the slander forever at rest. "You seek
(said he to Scott) to create the belief that you were
drawn from your quiet position in a bureau of this
department, and assigned to the command of our
armies in Mexico for the purpose of being sacrificed; in other words, that the Government, after
preferring you to any other of the gallant generals
within the range of its choice, had labored to frus-
trate its own plans, to bring defeat on its own
armies, and to involve itself in ruin and disgrace
for an object so unimportant in its bearing upon
public affairs. A charge so entirely preposterous,
so utterly repugnant to all the probabilities of
human conduct, calls for no refutation." The re-
vival of the calumny shows that Governor Marcy
relied too much upon the good sense of the people;
and I propose now to supply the proof which he
disdained to offer.

In entering upon the task of refuting the accusation, I am met with the difficulty that no evidence
whatever has been offered in support of it. In the
nature of things a negative is impossible of direct
proof; and the usual method of proving that a thing
is not so, is by contradicting the evidence that it
is so. But the charge that Scott was sent out to
slaughter Taylor is supported only by the affirma-

tion that there is "no doubt" of it; and the allegation that Scott said he had been promised reinforcements and supplies which were never sent, is not supported even by that kind of corroboration. Such a mode of fastening a great crime upon respectable men surprised me not a little, until, long after this article was in hand, I met with the following extracts from a panegyric upon General Grant, which sheds some light upon his method of dealing with truth.

"To any one who knew much of Grant's peculiar mental traits it would be quite easily believed that when Grant had asserted either matter of fact or opinion, he quite naively assumed that the burden of proof was on him who questioned it. * * * * His quiet but undoubting confidence in himself was one of the conditions of his great success."*

One great advantage which this peculiar mental trait secures to its possessor is, that if the person whom he assails happens to be in his grave—as is the case in the present instance—the burden of proof is very apt to rest where puts it. Nevertheless I feel impelled to undertake the task of vindication even with the burden, and am confident I shall be able, even thus handicapped, to make my case clear.

* Quoted in Notes on the Personal Memoirs of P. H. Sheridan by Brevet Lt. Col. C. McClellan, page 29.

The Myth in Chrysalis.

The first allegation in order of time is that
General Taylor was " selected for his lack of political ambition " to command the first army in Mexico;
the "army of occupation," as it was called.   The
fact is that General Taylor was, when so selected,
and had been for the five years preceding, stationed
in Louisiana with a considerable military force, in
command of the first military department, com-
prising five Southwestern States ; and he was, by
perhaps a thousand miles, nearer to the threatened
frontier than any other department commander
who could have been spared for the same duty.
He had also commanded with success in the Black
Hawk and Seminole wars.   But General Grant's
"quiet but undoubting confidence in himself"
assures him he knows the true ground of the selec-
tion, and that it was for political ends.

It is insinuated that Taylor would have been sus-
pended after his victories had begun to render him
formidable in the political field, but that "all the
capable officers of the requisite rank belonged to
the opposition."   Now, the *Army Register* for
1846, page 28, contains a list of general officers,
twelve in number; in the order of rank, Taylor is
eleventh on the list.   Among these are Jesup,
Wool, and Worth, all Democrats so far as they had

any politics; all capable officers, and all of them served in the field in the Mexican war. Wool and Worth won distinction at the head of troops; and Jesup was at the front as Quartermaster-General. He had commanded in the Seminole war, and in the Creek troubles in Alabama. Before the President promoted Taylor over all the brigadiers, Jesup and Wool were his seniors, and if either of them had been sent to join him with reinforcements after his first victories, Taylor would have been superseded by mere operation of law, and a Democrat placed in command.

Now, let us see what was the course of the Administration toward Taylor. The moment the news of his first victories reached Washington the President gave him the brevet of major general (No. 1)—the highest rank in the Army—and gave him the command of all the forces then and thereafter to be directed against Mexico (No. 3). A democratic Congress voted him thanks and a gold medal, and created an additional office of major general, to which the President forthwith appointed him. The President is represented as refusing to give the command in Mexico to General Scott, lest he should make political capital, and yet he did his best to enhance the effect of Taylor's victories by heaping honors upon him. In addition, he addressed General Taylor a letter, in terms of the most glowing praise, and directed him to publish it to the army under his command, and thus to the whole country (No. 1).

This was on the 30th of May, 1846. Immediately thereafter, June 8th (No. 2), the Secretary of War consulted him as to the advisability of "striking a blow at the city of Mexico,"and asked whether it could be reached from the north; and, without waiting for a reply, the Secretary on the 9th of July (No. 5) suggested it could be best reached by way of Vera Cruz, which could be easily captured, and from which port, he said, a fine carriage road led to the capital. And he asked General Taylor's views as to such an expedition. To the first letter Taylor replied under date of July 2d (No. 4), and to the second letter, under date of August 1st (No. 6). He said the city of Mexico could not be reached from the north and by land, and with regard to the suggested expedition by way of Vera Cruz he could give no opinion, either as to its practicability or as to the force it would require. "The Department of War" (he said) "must be much better informed than" he. But he thought his army could reach San Luis Potosi, and had no doubt the occupation of that city would bring proposals of peace.

The Secretary of War then proposed, September 2d (No. 7), to capture Tampico, which General Taylor had said "would be important to the occupation of San Luis Potosi," 150 miles distant, and asked General Taylor's views as to that enterprise. This letter was intercepted by the enemy and did not reach General Taylor. On the 22d of September (No. 9), the Secretary wrote that it was proposed to take Tampico, and that to save time General Patterson (who was on the Rio Grande while Taylor had advanced far into the interior) would be directed to hold himself in readiness to proceed immediately unless his withdrawal would interfere with General Taylor's operations. In reply, October 12th (No. 10), General Taylor briefly said that the attack on Tampico would be contrary to the convention which he had entered into on the capture of Monterey, and by which he had agreed not to advance beyond a certain point for eight weeks ; and three days later, in a letter dated October 15th (No. 11), he entered fully into the subject of an advance into the provinces of Tamaulipas and San Luis Potosi, which he discouraged, and begged that at least his army might not be required to co-operate in it just then. Continuing, he said:

"It may be expected that I should give my views as to the policy of occupying a defensive line, to which I have above alluded. I am free to confess that in view of the difficulties and expense attending a movement into the heart of the country, and particularly in view of the unsettled and revolutionary character of the Mexican Government, the occupation of such a line seems to me the best course that can be adopted. The line taken might either be that on which we propose to insist as the boundary between the republics—say the Rio Grande —or the line to which we have advanced, viz., the Sierra Madre, including Chihuahua and Santa Fe. * * * Should the Government determine to strike a decisive blow at Mexico, it is my opinion that the force should land near Vera Cruz or Alvarado; and after establishing a secure depot, march thence on the capital. The amount of troops required for this service would not fall short in my judgment of 25,000 men, of which at least 10,000 to be regular troops.''

And then later on he said:

''I feel it due to my position and to the service to record my protest against the manner in which the Department has sought to make an important detachment from my command, specifically indicating not only the general officers, but to a considerable extent the troops, that were to compose it. While I remain in command of the army against Mexico, and am, therefore, justly held responsible by the Government and the country for the conduct of its operations, I must claim the right of organizing all detachments from it, and regulating the time and manner of their service. Above all do I consider it important that the Department of War should refrain from corresponding directly with my subordinates, and communicating orders and instructions on points which, by all military precept and practice, pertain exclusively to the General in chief command.''

Before this letter could reach Washington, the Secretary wrote the General on the 22d of October (No. 12) that the expedition against Vera Cruz was determined on if he could spare the necessary force ; and, if so, he might organize it under the command of General Patterson. In reply, November 12th, (No. 14) General Taylor thought the capture of Vera Cruz should not be attempted with less than 10,000 men ; 4,000 might probably effect a landing and carry the city, but they could do no more and might be overpowered by a large force of the enemy. After capturing Tampico, for which he was preparing, he could spare 4,000 men, but the rest must come from the States. Tampico was soon after captured by the navy alone.

Now, let us consider the situation. General Taylor had advanced 125 miles beyond the Rio Grande —to Saltillo—and considered it important to hold that position. Under the most favorable circumstances an exchange of letters required six weeks ; a longer time was usual, and letters were liable to be intercepted by the enemy, as they had been more than once and their bearers killed. He was in command of all the troops everywhere in Mexico, and he claimed the right to make all detachments from his army, designate the officers to command them, and to regulate the time and manner of their

service. On this he had insisted in his letter of
October 15th (No. 11), and he repeated it in letters of
December 14th (No. 21) and December 26th (No. 25).
The Administration had in September proposed to
Mexico to open negotiations for peace, and Mexico
had refused to entertain the proposition (No. 9).
It was clear that no amount of warring in the re-
mote and thinly settled provinces would compel
Mexico to entertain proposals for peace, and that
an expedition against the capital was of absolute
necessity. But how could General Taylor direct
that expedition while he was at such a distance at
once from the base of supplies and from the scene
of operations? And then he had never approved
of the expedition; still less intimated a willingness
to command it. And indeed, if, as General Grant
doubted not, General Taylor "looked upon the
enemy as the aggrieved party," there was good
reason for his reluctance to advise or to command
the expedition, or even to have his army engaged
in it.*

On the other hand, General Scott was anxious
for service in the field. In May he had applied for
the command of Taylor's army—"the principal
army against Mexico"— then (May 27), "or at any
better time (the President) may be pleased to designate," and on September 12th (No. 8) he had re-

---

* General Grant declares that the way in which the war was
forced upon Mexico was wholly unjustifiable, pp. 54, 55.

minded the President of his said application, and remarked that he had reason to believe his presence at the head of the army in the field, in accordance with his rank, was "neither unexpected nor undesired by that gallant and distinguished commander." Six weeks later he had become a convert to the scheme of an expedition to the capital *via* Vera Cruz. In a memoir of October 27th (No. 13) he said: "To conquer a peace I am now persuaded that we must take the city of Mexico or place it in imminent danger of capture, and mainly through the city of Vera Cruz." And in a subsequent memoir of November 12th (No. 15) he said: "Until recently I had concurred in the opinion of others that Mexico might be compelled to propose reasonable terms of accommodation by the time we had conquered the advantages our arms have now obtained." And in subsequent memoirs of November 16th (No. 16) and 21st (No. 17) he recommended the withdrawal of more than half of Taylor's army for the expedition of Vera Cruz, and urged its practicability. It has been shown above that the Department had long before come to a decision on the subject, and that the only question was whether the requisite force could be had, and that, in turn, depended upon the number that Taylor could spare. Scott calculated that Taylor would have before long 27,500 men under his command; he thought 14,000 of these could be spared for the Vera Cruz expedition, leaving 13,500 for the advance on San Luis Potosi. "To meet this double invasion (he said) Mexico must either divide her forces and increase our chances of success on both lines, or double her forces on one and leave the other comparatively open to our advance."

And so ultimately it turned out. Mexico concentrated her forces against Taylor and suffered a crushing defeat at Buena Vista; but acting a little more vigorously than Scott perhaps expected, Santa Anna came upon Taylor before he had received the reinforcements which were to make his army up to 13,500. But in justice to Scott, it must be said, and presently will be shown, that he did not intend Taylor should advance until he should have received those reinforcements.

On the 18th of November the President, in person, communicated to General Scott his orders to take command of the army in Mexico, which were, a few days later, embodied in written instructions from the Secretary of War, dated November 23, 1846 (No. 19). On the same day Scott had handed the Secretary a draft of the instructions which he desired to be given him by the Department (No. 18), which, however, the Department did not adopt. In view of the charges I am considering, it may be well here to note that in the latter Scott desired to be instructed to organize and conduct an expedition against Vera Cruz, and to draw troops from Taylor's army, only "taking care to leave with him a sufficient force to defend Monterey and to keep his line of communication open, say, to Camargo and thence down the Rio Grande to its mouth." This passage shows that he knew he was expected not to endanger Taylor; and I will anticipate the course of my narrative to say that six weeks after Scott left Washington the Secretary, hearing disquieting rumors respecting the concentration of a Mexican force in Taylor's front, wrote General Scott, under date of January 4, 1847 (No. 29), communicating his anxiety and making all the suggestions a civilian could make on such a subject. Among these was an opinion that Taylor ought not to extend his line to Saltillo, in which Scott concurred and so wrote to Taylor January 26th (No. 32). Again, on the 22d of March, the Secretary, having heard of Santa Anna's advance, but not yet of his defeat, wrote to General Scott (No. 37) of his anxiety, and urged him to provide for Taylor's safety even, if necessary, by sending back troops from Vera Cruz.

I think these extracts will convince every fair-minded man that Governor Marcy, so far from desiring that General Taylor should be slaughtered, was doing all he could do to secure his safety. I proceed now to speak of Scott's conduct towards Taylor.

LeavingWashington November 23d General Scott repaired to New York, whence he addressed a confidential letter to Taylor, dated November 25th (No. 20), in which he stated his expectation of being by the 23d of December at Camargo on the Rio Grande (" within easy corresponding distance of you "), and suggested that they might later on meet " somewhere in the interior of Mexico." He regretted he should have to reduce Taylor temporarily to the necessity of standing on the defensive ; his own expedition could not be delayed, because he must take Vera Cruz before the yellow fever season set in. But more volunteers had been called for; Congress had been asked for more regulars, "and long before the spring (March) it is probable you will be in a condition to resume offensive operations." To this letter Taylor replied in one marked unofficial (No. 25), in which he said " at all times and places I shall be happy to receive your orders, and to hold myself and troops at your disposition." From New Orleans, and again on arriving at Camargo, where Scott found that Taylor was at Victoria, some 200 miles to the south, he addressed Taylor letters under dates of December 20, 1846 (No. 22), and January 3, 1847 (No. 27), in which he explained more fully his plans, and in the last, repeated that Taylor would be " reduced for a time to the strict defensive." On the same day he wrote to General Butler (No. 28), ordering him, " without waiting to hear from General Taylor," to send to the Brazos for embarkation to Vera Cruz about 9,000 men. Notwithstanding General Taylor had only a week before placed himself and troops at the disposition of General Scott, and Scott was his superior officer, General Taylor declared he was "mortified and outraged" at his interference with his command, and strongly resented it in a letter to General Scott, dated January 15, 1847 (No. 31). He complained that he had been kept in ignorance of the designs of the Government, and had evidently lost its confidence, and he would have been much better satisfied had he been relieved of command or allowed to retire from the field; and the expectation which seemed to be entertained that he could assume offensive operations by March or even May was "preposterous." Even to hold a defensive line he had less than a thousand regulars and a volunteer force mostly of new levies, while an army of more than 20,000 men was in his front. He did not say he could not hold the defensive line. On the contrary, in a letter written some days later, January 27th (No. 33), to the Adjutant General, with instructions to submit it to the Secretary of War, to be by him laid before the President, he said: "The force with which I am left in this quarter, though greatly deficient in regular troops, will doubtless enable me to hold the position now occupied."

The sum of the matter is, that whereas Scott was directed to leave Taylor enough troops to defend him behind the walls of Monterey, which was the most advanced position he was expected or desired to maintain, he in fact left him strong enough to meet the enemy in the open field, fifty miles in advance of that position, and to gain a great and decisive victory.

At a later period, in April, 1847, reinforcements were to be sent forward to Scott to enable him to advance upon Mexico. They were by previous arrangement sent to the Brazos, a point within the limits of his command, and there came under his orders. In the instructions given by General Scott, April 25th (No. 39), to the commanding officer there, to forward them on to Vera Cruz, he made it "conditional on the safety of the line of the Rio Grande," and left it to his "own sound judgment to determine on the spot" whether that line would be too much exposed by the withdrawal of the troops in question.

On the whole, I conclude that General Scott was as little desirous to expose Taylor to slaughter and defeat as the President and Secretary were that he should do so.

I pass now to the second branch of the subject— the treatment of General Scott by the Administration.

It is charged that the President and Secretary of

War, in pursuance of a plan to disgrace General Scott, withheld one-half of the men and munitions of war which he had estimated to be necessary for the success of his expedition, and which they had promised him with expressions of "sincere good wishes." And the charge is repeated in connection with the expedition to Vera Cruz, for which, it is said, Scott had less than 12,000 men when he was promised a much larger force.

The only estimates of troops ever made by General Scott were in his four memoirs of October 27th and November 12th, 16th, and 21st (Nos. 13, 15, 16, and 17). In these he stated that "to place the capture of both places beyond the probability of a failure" (both places, the city and castle) "an army of at least 10,000 men" was indispensable. Personally he would be willing to attempt it with a smaller army, but doubted whether the Government ought to risk it with less than 12,000, perhaps 15,000 men. In the instructions hereinbefore referred to, which he drafted and proposed the Secretary should give him (No. 18), the Secretary was to tell him that though he (Scott) thought 15,000 not an unreasonable number of troops for the expedition, and 10,000 the minimum, "you are yet of opinion that the expedition ought to go forward even with the first 8,000 men that may be embarked off Point Isabel, sooner than incur the danger of losing your men and object by the yellow fever in consequence of

waiting too long for either of the larger numbers
you have mentioned." The Secretary declined to
give the instructions asked or to name any force
whatever, but, as we shall presently see, left it to
Scott himself to decide what force he could take
from Taylor, and what he should take.

And in the first letter he wrote Taylor after
reaching New Orleans, dated December 20th (No.
22), General Scott said that while 15,000 men were
desirable, I "am now inclined to move forward to
the attack should I be able to assemble the 5,000
regulars, and, say, three of volunteers." We have
seen that Taylor thought the city alone might
possibly be taken by 4,000 men. Scott, from his
draft of 23d November, and his letter of 20th December, appears to have determined to make the
attempt if he could get no more than 8,000 men.
And in these calculations he expected to encounter
20,000 or 30,000 men on landing at Vera Cruz, or
even double that number if Mexico could arm so
many; and to land, "no doubt, under heavy fire"
(No. 15).

In the instructions which he drafted for the Secretary to give him, he was to be directed to organize
an expedition against Vera Cruz, and to make up
the expeditionary force from the army of General
Taylor and from nine regiments of volunteers which
had recently been called for, but had not yet been
organized. The Secretary declined to give him

such unconditional orders. In the instructions which he did give (No. 19) he directed Scott to organize the expedition, "if on arriving at the theatre of action you shall deem it to be practicable. It is not proposed (he continues) to control your operations by definite and positive instructions, but you are left to prosecute them as your judgment, under a full view of all the circumstances, shall dictate." And finally, he hoped General Scott would have the requisite force to accomplish the objects in view, but "of this you must be the judge when preparations are made, and the time for action has arrived."

The sources of supply stated in the draft of instructions were the nine new regiments of volunteers and Taylor's army in the field, which last by his seniority of rank and his assignment to command became absolutely his own, whether he went on to Vera Cruz or not. The volunteers he thought might begin to arrive "off Point Isabel say about the middle of January." "Such (he makes the Secretary say to him) are your own (Scott's) calculations." Thus, then, a large army was actually given him, and a force had been called for in addition, which he, knowing perhaps better than the Secretary, the process of organizing volunteers calculated would be with him in January. He expected to take from the two, 14,000 men, as stated in his memoir of November 16th (No. 16), and he still expected so many when he reached New Orleans; for he wrote General Butler to send him from Taylor's army 9,100 men, and he expressed his intention elsewhere to take five regiments, say 5,000 men of the new volunteers; but for reasons which I do not find stated, the whole, when assembled, amounted not to 14,000, but only to 12,000 men, and with these he proceeded to Vera Cruz, landing with no enemy to oppose him, and without hearing a hostile shot except from the castle, and he, of course, took care to land far beyond the range of its guns.

General Grant says Captain Alburtis was killed in landing. General Scott in his dispatch of March 12th says the landing was effected "without accident or loss," and that Alburtis and many others were killed two days after "in extending the line of investments around the city."

It is manifest, from the circumstances and conditions of the case, that it is impossible that General Scott could have had the promise of any troops whatever. He was given the actual command of all the troops in service, and as to the volunteers all the President could do was to call for them, which he certainly had done before Scott was assigned to command, and the orders for sending them forward were given by General Scott himself (No. 24). And then, in all the correspondence between Scott and the Department, we look in vain for any reference, either by Scott or the Secretary, to any promise by the Department of troops, or, indeed, of anything else. In his draft of instructions General Scott speaks of what he had recommended, but never of what the President had promised. And what is conclusive is this: During the campaign in Mexico he got into difficulties with his subordinates, and, as the President would not court-martial them, he asked to be relieved; and after the city was taken and the enemy subdued he was relieved. This and some other things stung him to frenzy, and he sat down and drew a long indictment against the Department (No. 43), which I shall have occasion to review at length, charging the Secretary with numerous manifestations of hostility to him, and sundry neglects and disappointments; but never once did he say that the Secretary had made or had broken a promise. The only place in that long letter where the word "promised" is used is in a misquotation from one of his own letters, in which the actual word was "informed."

As for troops for subsequent operations, it is sufficient to say that the largest number ever estimated by General Taylor for the campaign against the capital was 25,000, and the largest number ever named by General Scott in his various memoirs or elsewhere was 20,000, and though with his usual caution he added that more might be needed, he named no greater number. Now, he must have had in all 36,000 or 37,000 men; for he had in November, 1847, 32,156 men, as stated in the Adjutant General's report and the annual report of the Secretary of War at the next session (Nos. 51, 50), and he had lost many men in battle, and had discharged at least 3,700 volunteers after reaching the interior (No. 50). So that as regards men, it is simply impossible that the President and Secretary could have ever made any promises to General Scott that were not fulfilled, or any promises at all, or that General Scott ever could have said they did ; and finally it is certain that they gave him nearly twice as many men as he had ever asked for.

I have had occasion to say that General Scott did, in fact, make certain charges against the President and Secretary, and I must add that these charges were somewhat of the nature of those which General Grant has repeated (No. 43). In all essential features, however, they were false, and their falsity was exposed in an immediate reply by the Secretary of War (No. 44). General Scott's letter and Governor Marcy's reply were printed by Congress in the same document (Doc. 59, H. R., 1847–8), and I think I may say that only very careless reading or wilful blindness could fail to see that the refutation was perfect. The friends of General

Scott had been content for thirty years to let his mistake lie in the quiet obscurity of a Congressional document, and his political opponents, mindful of his great services to his country, have felt no disposition to disturb its rest. But to the politician the individual is as nought in comparison with the party, and the soldier is accustomed to sacrifice friends that foes may perish with them. And there is abundant evidence in the "Personal Memoirs" that General Grant cared nothing for General Scott, besides the disservice he has done him in producing him as a witness against Governor Marcy, and most unjustifiably making the issue that either Scott lied or Marcy was a traitor; for that, in plain words, is just as General Grant puts it. I hope to show that he has not the authority of General Scott for any such position. The internal evidence is conclusive that General Grant's authority for what Scott said is derived exclusively from Scott's published dispatches, and particularly from the accusatory letter above referred to, and in disposing of the charges made in that letter I dispose of those made by General Grant on General Scott's alleged authority. But it is a matter of sincere regret to me that this scheme of defence renders inevitable the exposure of some of the errors and weaknesses of General Scott, who, in spite of glaring faults, had some great and many estimable qualities.

General Scott, in conduct and conversation, was as pure as a woman, and strangely enough, great soldier as he certainly was, his weaknesses were distinctively feminine. His pride in his fine figure was manifested only too often. His fondness for display and finery have been shown up in the Personal Memoirs,* and his dispatches contain examples of an aimless querulousness, not perhaps elsewhere to be found in masculine correspondence. In his reports he bewails the delays and mishaps due to the elements on a stormy coast and in a stormy season, and disclaims his responsibility for them in a tone that suggests the responsibility must rest somewhere. And so in his accusatory letter he complains that only so many supplies came, implying, but not at all asserting, that others ought to have come. It is these incomplete complaints that have misled General Grant's eager credulity, and he has formulated them in the shape which he would fain make us believe General Scott intended to give them; that is, that what mishaps General Scott met with, the Administration had undertaken to avert, and had wilfully failed to do so; and what he failed to receive, the Administration had undertaken to supply, and had purposely withheld.

---

* This is done with a touch of humor, notwithstanding General Grant's Scotch blood. And there is, too, a spice of sarcasm in his apophthegm, that nothing so popularizes a candidate for high *civil position* as *military victories*.

There were four, and only four, complaints in that letter having any reference to "men and material." Two of them are contained in the following paragraph :

"The embarkation was delayed in whole or in part from the 15th of January to the 9th of March, leaving, it was feared, not half the time needed for the reduction of Vera Cruz and its castle before the return of the yellow fever. But half the surf-boats came at all, and of the siege train and ordnance stores only about one-half had arrived [at Vera Cruz] when the Mexican flags were replaced by those of the United States on those formidable places [the city and castle]. We succeeded at last in reaching the point of attack in the midst of frightful northers, by means in great part of trading craft, small and hazardous, picked up accidently at the Brazos and Tampico, and when the army got ashore its science and valor had to supply all deficiencies in heavy guns, mortars, and ordnance stores " (No. 43).

This paragraph contains the only mention made in the letter of surf boats, siege train, and ordnance stores, and the letter nowhere indicates how many or much ought to have arrived, or who was responsible for their failure to arrive. But as the whole letter is devoted to an arraignment of the Administration, the casual reader would understand that the failure was to be imputed to the War Department; yet General Scott, while certainly willing to be so understood, does not say so ; and it is left for General Grant to boldly interpret it into an allegation that the Secretary had promised him a certain supply of guns and ordnance stores, and furnished only half.

Now, as it turned out, the surf boats, which were constructed at a cost of $130,000, solely for the purpose of landing the army at Vera Cruz on the single occasion, were not needed at all; and of the siege train and ordnançe stores twice as many mortars and twenty times as many shells reached him at Vera Cruz before the surrender as he had occasion to use.   He was enabled to complain, with truth, that only about half had been received by having asked for five times as many guns and forty times as many shells as were needed, and twice as many of both as could possibly be made and delivered in time to be of use.

But to be more specific, General Scott expected that on arriving at Vera Cruz he would find a Mexican army of at least 25,000 men ready to oppose his landing (No. 15.)   He therefore asked for 140 surf boats, so that he could put ashore at a single instant 5,000 men, who, under cover of the fire of the fleet, could make good their footing on land.   These boats he thought would cost $200 apiece; in fact they cost $960 (No. 44).   And they were all promptly forwarded to him, for he mentions in a letter of February 28 (No. 36), that General Jones, the Adjutant General, had written him that *all* had been shipped. But, as I have said, no surf boats were needed at all, because there was no enemy on the beach, or within a hundred miles of the beach, except the small garrison of Vera Cruz, who wisely kept within their walls. The whole army could have been landed in the boats of the fleet. But General Scott took no risks.

As regards the siege train and ordnance stores, it was General Scott's business to order them, and he said, on the 16th of November, that he would do so on that day (No. 16), and he ordered 50 large mortars and 4,000 tons—say eighty or one hundred thousand—shells (No. 44). When the Chief of Ordnance received this requisition he at once pronounced it "preposterous." The shells, he said, were enough to bury Vera Cruz in iron, and he knew the vast order could not be filled in time. Nevertheless, as was his duty, he submitted it to the Secretary, and the Secretary ordered that it be complied with "as far as practicable" (No. 44). All the mortars were made and shipped, and 67,000 shells, as shown by the report of the Ordnance Department accompanying the President's annual message of December, 1847. General Scott says about half were received. Half would be 25 mortars and at least 40,000 shells ; but his report from Vera Cruz (No. 45) shows that only 23 mortars reached him, and there must have been, if not

40,000, then 30,000, shells. That all did not reach
him the Secretary attributed to the fact that at that
day the iron foundries depended for their heavy
freighting upon the rivers and other water-ways of
the interior, and these, in the dead of winter, were
frozen (No. 44). But 23 mortars and at least 30,000
shells reached Vera Cruz in time for the siege (No.
45).

As soon as ten of these mortars were placed in
battery, the firing upon the city began, and these
ten mortars, with the aid of two batteries of 24-
pounders—one of these constructed, armed, and
worked by the sailors of the fleet—accomplished
the capture of Vera Cruz and its castle. (Nos. 45
and 46). And these several batteries threw alto-
gether 2,500 solid shot and shells (No. 46); so that
if the mortars were fired as rapidly as the guns
(which they were not), the ten mortars would have
thrown 1,140 shells, and the twelve other guns
1,360 solid shot. And the conclusion is that General Scott, in asking for 50 mortars and 80,000 shells,
asked for five times as many mortars and seventy
times as many shells as he found need for. And
when he said the science and valor of the army
"had to supply all deficiencies in heavy guns, mortars, and ordnance stores," he actually had on hand
twice as many mortars and thirty times as many
shells, and probably six times as many heavy guns,
as he found use for. As to the heavy guns, indeed

the information is not so specific.   Forty-four were issued according to the ordnance report above quoted, and he must have asked for them, but he had only six in battery.   He never complained that any had failed to reach him.   The other 38 may have been lying on the beach with the unused mortars, while valor and skill supplied their place.

Another charge, to which great prominence is given in the letter of complaint, is that ten transports, which General Scott had requested to have sent out in ballast from Atlantic ports, to carry troops from the Brazos and Tampico to Vera Cruz, and which the Secretary had ordered to be so sent, never came.   " Relying upon them, confidently, (he says in No. 43), the embarkation was delayed in whole or in part at the Brazos and Tampico from the 15th of January to the 9th of March, leaving, it was feared, not half the time needed for the reduction of Vera Cruz and its castle before the return of the yellow fever." (No. 43.)   The order had indeed been given, and the vessels never came ! but why ?

" Forseeing at Washington (he says in No. 43) that from the great demands of commerce at the moment, it would be difficult, if not impossible, to take up, perhaps at any price, a sufficient number of vessels at New Orleans and Mobile to transport the regiments of my expedition from the Rio Grande frontier to Vera Cruz," he had made the request, and the order was given. But General Scott at Washington was not in a position to know as well as the Quartermaster General at New Orleans, what vessels could be had at the latter point. He had himself advised that the ships "be not chartered until the troops are known to be nearly in position to embark" (No. 16), and the Secretary, while out of abundant caution, giving the order December 15th, had previously (December 11th) written to General Jesup at New Orleans to know whether it would be necessary to send out vessels in ballast, which he said would be enormously expensive.

When this letter reached New Orleans, General Scott was there, and saw and read it; and in a letter to the Secretary (No. 23) so informed him, and remarked upon certain matters concerning transportation. General Jesup replied (No. 26): "Transportation can be provided here for all the troops that may be drawn from the army under the command of General Taylor. * * * The public transports * * * it is estimated, will carry 3,000 men with all their supplies. Vessels can be chartered here on favorable terms for any additional transportation that may be required." General Scott saw this letter before it was sent, and marked on it "read," and noted his concurrence in certain recommendations made on another subject. On receipt of this letter by the Secretary, he, of course, countermanded his order to send vessels around to New Orleans in ballast. On the 26th of January, when, according to his letter of complaint, he had been waiting eleven days—since the 15th—for the ten vessels, General Scott wrote to the Secretary (No. 32): "The Quartermaster General (Brevet Major General Jesup) at New Orleans has, I find, taken all proper measures, with judgment and promptitude, to provide everything depending on his department for the dispatch and success of my expedition. Transports, casks filled with water, &c., &c., are accordingly expected to arrive here [the Brazos] and off Tampico before the 7th of the next month." Not a word is said of the ten vessels, and no mention is made of any delay.

On the 29th General Scott wrote to General Patterson at Tampico (No. 34): "Transports have been taken up at New Orleans for all the troops who are to compose my expedition, and embark here [Brazos] and at Tampico."

On the 12th of January (No. 30) he had written to General Brooke, in command at New Orleans, that the troops who were to embark at Brazos and Tampico would not "reach those points till late in the present month—say about the 25th." In the same letter he directed General Brooke to take particular care in causing all ships which were to

join him to be provided with fuel and water for
sixty or ninety days. "The water of the Rio
Grande [he added] is not good for drinking, and
there would be great difficulty in obtaining it.
Spare casks of Mississippi water on board ships
without troops may be easily shifted to the transports with men and horses."

If there was any delay, some of it was due to this
order.   For on February 1st he wrote from Brazos
to Captain Saunders, of the Navy (No. 35): "I may
be detained here several days longer waiting for
the transports to receive the troops in this neighbor-
hood and at Tampico, and those ships I know are
detained at New Orleans, waiting for water casks,
in the hands of coopers."   This is all that he says
about the detention or the cause of it.   But how
utterly impossible it renders his allegation that he
delayed the embarkation waiting for the ten vessels
to arrive.

But this is not all.   The delay is said to have
extended from the 15th of January to the 9th of
March.   Now, I have quoted above, from his letter
of 12th January, that the troops to embark at
Brazos and Tampico were not expected to reach
those points before the 25th, and other reports show
that they did not.   Then, on the 9th of March,
when they are said to have embarked at Brazos,
the whole army landed at Vera Cruz.   When they
embarked I cannot state, nor is it material, but be-

fore the 9th of March they had crossed the Gulf of Mexico, in sailing vessels, "in the midst of frightful northers," and had in the meantime rendezvoused at Lobos. General Grant says the voyage was tedious, and "many of the troops were on shipboard thirty days." So it is certain they did not land at Vera Cruz on the same day they left Brazos.

I have already said that in none of General Scott's letters, not even in that devoted to an enumeration of "the neglects, disappointments, injuries, and rebukes which [had] been inflicted" upon him by the War Department (No. 43), is it alleged that any troops had been promised him by the War Department; still less that he did not receive all that he expected. He did, however, complain that certain troops under General Cadwallader, which he had expected to be sent to Vera Cruz, had been sent to Brazos, and that the want of them had crippled his operations. To this Governor Marcy replied that he had given no orders on the subject; that before General Scott left for Mexico he had himself arranged that all the troops sent to him should report at the Brazos, which place was within the limits of his command, and it was in pursuance of that arrangement that they were sent thither. It is true that in advising General Scott of their departure for that point (No. 37), the Secretary had spoken of the reports of General Taylor's critical position, and the succor which the troops would be in a position to afford him; for though this was a month after the battle of Buena Vista, intelligence of it had not reached Washington. General Scott, in acknowledging the receipt of this letter (No. 40), took no exception to what he afterwards called the "diversion" of those troops; and, in ordering them on to Vera Cruz, he made the order conditional upon their not being needed by General Taylor. A year later, when he was seeking subjects of complaint, this diversion, the effect solely of his own orders, was made to play a most important part. He said a soldier [only] could imagine his distress on hearing these troops had been diverted to the Rio Grande, for had General Cadwallader not been so delayed, he believed he could have taken Mexico in June at one-fifth the loss he afterwards sustained in August (No. 43). I have no doubt he could have done so, and that his loss would have been, not a fifth, but only a twenty-fifth of what he sustained in August. And not only this, but it is certain that without General Cadwallader's troops he could have done the same. For after he had heard in April that General Cadwallader's troops were at the Brazos, and after he had ordered that officer to remain there if he should find it necessary (No. 39), General Scott discharged and sent home 3,700 veteran volunteers who had yet from four to seven weeks to serve, twice the time that, three months later, proved necessary for the taking of the city (No. 47).

And now to the proof of this:

On the 23d of April he wrote to Colonel Wilson at Vera Cruz (No. 38): "We already occupy Perote and shall soon occupy Puebla. *Indeed, we might safely take possession of Mexico without a loss, perhaps, of one hundred men.* Our dangers and difficulties are the rear." Santa Anna was eighty miles in the rear of Scott, who was between him and the Capital, and he was "without arms, magazines or military chest" (No. 40). The Government was preparing to leave the city (No. 39). But having sent home the volunteers, Scott sat down at Puebla for three months, while Santa Anna made his way to the Capital, and, as General Scott says, "had time to collect, to treble, to organize and discipline his forces, and also to erect numerous and powerful defences, with batteries" (No. 43). So that, instead of 100 men, he lost 2,703 in taking the city.

Let me make this still plainer. After Santa Anna had been allowed three months to make his way to the Capital and fortify it in the manner stated, General Scott, resumed the offensive on the 7th of August, fought several battles, and had the city at his mercy on the 20th. In his despatch of August 28th, giving an account of a series of battles fought on the 20th, and several victories won on that day, he says : "After so many victories, we might, with little additional loss, have occupied the Capital the same evening." But he granted an armistice. Now the force with which he achieved the victories in August was 10,738 men (No. 49). The force which he had under his command in May, before he discharged the volunteers, must have been 9,000 men.* It is obvious that Santa Anna's 30,000 men and fortifications far more than counterbalanced the few hundreds by which General Scott had increased his force, and that he would have found it far easier to take the city in May, with 9,000 men (which he said he could do with the loss of 100 men), than he found it in August with 10,738 men, when his actual loss was 2,703 men, and he could have done it quicker. Or, if no quicker, he could have done it in fourteen days, the time actually required, while the volunteers had twenty-eight days or longer to serve.

Why he discharged the volunteers thus in advance of the expiration of their term, perhaps only a soldier can understand; but a politician might be pardoned for suspecting that Scott, who " was known to have political aspirations," might hope for the votes of men whom he thus released

---

* General Grant says nine or ten thousand (p. 135).

from an arduous and dangerous service. The reason he gave, that none of them would re-engage,
and that, if retained to the end of their terms,
they would have to pass through Vera Cruz during
the yellow fever season, may be true, but he could
have taken Mexico by the 20th of May $(6+14=20)$,
and the volunteers could have reached Vera Cruz
considerably in advance of the yellow fever, which ·
ordinarily arrives in June.

The rest of the complaints in the accusatory
letter refer mostly to the refusals of the President
to appoint or promote officers whom he had recommended, and to court-martial others, of whom he
had complained. But as these and a few others
do not concern the question of reinforcements and
supplies, I shall not report the replies which Governor Marcy made to them. There are, however,
two circumstances which shed such light upon the
character of the testimony which General Grant
has adduced against Governor Marcy, that the defence would be incomplete without noticing them
both.

In his letter of accusation General Scott says:

"Only four days were allowed me at Washington, where twenty might have been most advan-
tageously employed in the great bureaus, those of
the Chief Engineer, Chief of Ordnance, Chief

Quartermaster, and Chief Commissary of Subsistence." (No. 43.)

For answer to this, Governor Marcy quietly quoted a paragraph from the draft of instructions which Scott had requested the Secretary to address to him (No. 18). In this draft Scott desires the Secretary to say to him :

"I am pleased to learn from you that you have, in a very few days, already, through the general staff of the army here, laid a sufficient basis for the purposes with which you are charged, and that you now think it best to proceed at once to the southwest, in order to organize the largest number of troops that can be obtained in time for that most important expedition."

Thus, having applied in writing for orders to proceed to the front, and assigned as a reason that he had done all that was necessary at Washington, General Scott, in less than fifteen months thereafter, complained, also in writing, that he had not been allowed time in Washington to complete his preparations.

The remaining incident had perhaps a more unfortunate effect upon General Scott's military operations than any that I have mentioned, and yet it is not alluded to in his accusatory letter.

The President, in April, 1847, sent to Mexico Mr. N. P. Trist, chief clerk of the State Department, bearing a sealed dispatch addressed to the Mexican Minister of Foreign Relations, and an order from the War Department directing General Scott to have this despatch forwarded to its address by flag of truce. Mr. Trist was also entrusted with a copy of the sealed despatch, and a copy of the treaty which it was the purpose of that despatch to propose to the Mexican Government, and which, if accepted and duly ratified by Mexico, was to be followed by a suspension of hostilities. Mr. Trist was instructed to exhibit these copies to General Scott, and when the reply of the Mexican Government should be received, accepting and ratifying the treaty, to give General Scott information to that effect, in order that he might suspend hostilities, until the treaty could be submitted to the Senate for ratification on the part of the United States. (No. 42.)

On reaching Vera Cruz, Mr. Trist found an opportunity to forward the despatch and the order to General Scott, who was at Jalapa, and he followed on soon after. And there he received back from General Scott the sealed packet intended for the Mexican Minister of Foreign Affairs, with a letter in which General Scott positively refused to forward it, for sundry reasons, of which not the least potent was probably this: "I see [wrote General Scott No. 41] that the Secretary of War proposes to de-

grade me by requiring that I, the Commander of
this Army, shall defer to you, the chief clerk of the
State Department, the question of continuing or
discontinuing hostilities." And he claimed that
"armistice or no armistice is most peculiarly a military question," and that if the enemy should entertain the overtures, that question should be referred
to him.

Accordingly, when ready, he advanced upon the
City of Mexico, and after a succession of battles,
fought on the 20th of August, in all which he was
victorious, he granted the enemy an armistice with
a view to negotiate a peace. "After so many victories [writes General Scott, No. 48] we might, with
but little additional loss, have occupied the Capital
the same evening. But Mr. Trist, commissioner,
&c., as well as myself, had been admonished by
the best friends of peace," not to drive away the government, and, by taking the Capital, excite a spirit
of national desperation; and so he granted a military
armistice, of which the Mexicans availed themselves
with such diligence that when hostilities were resumed it cost General Scott a loss of 1,651 men before he could enter the city. The instructions of
the War Department were that hostilities should
cease only after negotiations should have been
brought to an end by the acceptance by Mexico
of the terms offered, and by the ratification by
Mexico of a treaty embodying them, whereas Gen-

eral Scott granted an armistice in order to enter upon negotiations, with the result that the negotiations were availed of by the Mexicans only to amuse the Americans, and cost them the heavy loss I have stated.

The reader will probably be surprised that General Scott adduced the authority of Mr. Trist on the "peculiarly military question" of armistice. I must, therefore, mention that after a correspondence, quite as acrid on Mr. Trist's part as on General Scott's, the "chief clerk of the Department of State" and "the Commander of this Army" had suddenly conceived the highest admiration for each other, and become fast friends. *

---

* This correspondence is a curiosity of literature. The writers contend which shall say the bitterest things, and each in his own proper style. The soldier is blunt and abusive; the diplomat smooth and sarcastic. Scott was tempted to return Trist's "farrago of insolence, conceit, and arrogance" to the writer, who, if he had "but an ambulatory guillotine, would be the personification of Danton, Marat, and St. Just all in one." Trist acknowledged "the amiable affability and gracious condescension" of Scott, whose "outward acts of respect for the Government" [he said] "bear the same relation to this sentiment which genuflections and upturnings of the eyes bear to religion." (Doc. 60, pp. 813-25, 996.)

THE EVOLUTION OF THE MYTH.

The evolution of the myth from the facts which constituted its chrysalis condition was effected solely by General Grant's imagination, aided, perhaps, somewhat by his logical faculty. If General Scott had received one-half the siege trains and ordnance stores, reason suggested there must have been a whole, and imagination added that the whole was the quantity promised. And when reason suggested there must have been a motive for withholding the half, imagination added that the motive was to disgrace Scott lest he should by success win a reputation that would render him a formidable rival for the Presidency. And in this way, and in this way only, is constructed against President Polk and his Secretary of War the charge of a crime exceeding in atrocity, I verily believe, any that history records—the crime, namely, of sending ten thousand men to death by pestilence and hostile arms, in order that their commander might be disgraced by the failure of the enterprise in which they were engaged.

Wisely did the great moralist of the last century and of our age say : " Among the calamities of war must be reckoned the diminution of a regard for truth." And the reason is not far to seek. The necessity of deceiving one's enemies and,

almost as often, one's friends, and the habit of look-
ing for success only to force and stratagem, and never
to justice or reason ; in short the fundamental conviction of the soldier that on whichever side may
be the right, "Heaven is always on the side of
the heaviest artillery, " must depreciate the warrior's estimate of the value of truth, deaden his
faculty of apprehending it, and render him in-
sensible to the necessity of taking it into account
as an element in the consideration of any subject.

CONCLUSION.

I feel that I have successfully achieved my task,
and no one who reads these pages with a mind
open to conviction will credit the charges made by
General Grant against President Polk and Secretary
Marcy. But this defence will not reach one in a
million of those who will read the charges. Speedy
oblivion will settle on this humble vindication,
while the great libel will take its place as a true
chapter in the History of the United States.

General Grant's sarcasm is as true as it is bitter.
The people honor the warrior who has triumphed
in fields of slaughter, though at home and in civil
war, more than the statesman who has rescued half
a continent from the dominion of superstition and
savagery, and given it to enlightened freedom and
peaceful industry.

References.

The following letters and reports are found in document No. 60, House of Representatives, 30th Congress, 1st Session, 1847–8:

No.		1846	Page
1	Secretary Marcy......................	May 30.	283
2	Same.........	June 8.	323
3	General Scott......................	June 12.	325
4	General Taylor........	July 2.	329
5	Secretary Marcy.........	July 9.	333
6	General Taylor.........,..............	Aug. 1.	336
7	Secretary Marcy......	Sept. 2.	339
8	General Scott............	Sept. 12.	372
9	Secretary Marcy.......	Sept. 22.	341
10	General Taylor......	Oct. 13.	350
11	Same.........	Oct. 15.	351
12	Secretary Marcy......................	Oct. 22.	363
13	General Scott......	Oct. 27.	1268
14	General Taylor......................	Nov. 12.	374
15	General Scott....	Nov. 12.	1270
16	Same............................	Nov. 16.	1273
17	Same......	Nov. 21.	1274
18	Same............................	Nov. 23.	1275
19	Secretary Marcy..............	Nov. 23.	836

The following reports are found in document No.
8, House of Representatives, Thirtieth Congress,
First Session, 1847–8. President's Annual Message.